THE BIRTH OF GOD

THE BIRTH OF GOD

Recovering the Mystery of Christmas

JOHN B. ROGERS, JR.

Abingdon Press

Nashville

THE BIRTH OF GOD
Recovering the Mystery of Christmas

Copyright © 1987 by Abingdon Press

This book is printed on acid-free paper.

Library of Congress Cataloging-in-Publication Data

Rogers, John B., 1941-
  The birth of God.

  Bibliography: p.
  1. Incarnation. I. Title.
        BT220.R65   1987   232'.1   87-1823
        ISBN 0-687-03554-6 (pbk.: alk. paper)

MANUFACTURED BY THE PARTHENON PRESS AT
NASHVILLE, TENNESSEE, UNITED STATES OF AMERICA

Contents

For my children, John and Ann DuPre,
who annually help their father
rediscover the mystery of Christmas

Preface

Certain European newspapers feature a regular weekly contest in the sports section. The paper prints an action photograph from a professional soccer match, but with the ball edited out of the picture. Readers are invited to cut out the photograph, guess where the ball belongs, draw it into the picture, and mail it in, with the paper awarding a cash prize for the best guess.

Shortly before his death, in a letter to his son, Markus, Karl Barth chose one such contest photograph to describe the situation in church and theology in the latter half of the twentieth century. Imagine the scene: Some players lying prostrate, as though overtaken by events, others leaping in apparent ecstasy, others gazing desperately about, looking to throw themselves into the game's latest development. Still others are gazing at themselves, or seem to be. One might add, from the perspective of the 1980s, that some players are attacking members of the opposing team. The goalkeeper appears frantic, as though some disaster were about to descend upon him; in the name of efficiency and good management, the "officials" are trying to get things organized. "But," as Barth said, "the ball is not in the picture, and no one knows where it is."[1]

To this confusion Almighty God addresses himself in Jesus Christ:

> "Behold, a virgin shall conceive and bear a son,
> and his name shall be called Emmanuel"
> (which means, God with us).

> *Matthew 1:23*

In other words, we do not have and have never had and shall never have to *put* God in the picture. On his own initiative, in his own good time, on his own terms, God comes to us *in person*—in *the* person of Jesus Christ. Christmas means the mystery that meets us at the heart and boundary of life is who we know it to be in Jesus Christ: personal, faithful, full of compassion, and abounding in steadfast love. Our problem, therefore, is not that we cannot find God, but that we cannot escape God. Nor can we finally thwart God's sovereign purpose or remove ourselves and our world beyond the limits of his invincible grace.

To preach the gospel at Christmas it to become intensely aware of the mystery of God's presence, of mystery and presence mediated in a human life. This book comes of one minister's attempt faithfully to proclaim and interpret this good, yet mysterious, news of "God with us."

Running through this volume is the dominant biblical theme of God's decision to be present with and for his people. Arising dramatically in the revelation of God's name to Moses at the burning bush (Exodus 3), this theme reaches back through the stories of the patriarchs to the very intention of God in creation itself. It reaches forward through the history of the people of God, through Torah [the law] and the prophets, to the life, death, and resurrection of Jesus Christ, who is God incarnate. In Christ's promise to be always with us to the close of the age (cf. Matthew 28:20), this theme becomes the message of the church to the world and the substance of its future hope beyond history (cf. Revelation 21:3 ff.). Indeed, the Emmanuel theme is one of several unifying themes in the Bible, around which a full-blown biblical theology may be constructed.[2]

In addition to biblical theology, this book draws on insights from historical and systematic theology. Preaching is a theological discipline. The proper content of preaching or proclamation, of course, is not theology, itself, but the gospel. However, if the gospel proclaimed is to be understood, believed, and obeyed, then serious theology is essential to the task of preaching. John H. Leith, who is an esteemed teacher and cherished friend, taught me long ago that "what cannot be thought through critically and expressed with reasonable clarity cannot demand the allegiance of a person's whole being. Understanding is necessary for . . . full commitment."[3] Theology is seldom usefully employed in preaching as an end in itself, but is rather a lens to a clearer vision of the gospel and a sharper focus of faith. Contributions from a variety of theological sources are, therefore, included in these pages, but no theologian is featured more prominently than Karl Barth, by whom I continue to be fed in my own vocation generally, and whose interpretive insights into the Christmas event I find especially helpful. This influence of Barth I acknowledge with gratitude and without apology.[4]

Theology is first cousin to poetry. So often poetry offers a simple, poignant expression of a deep truth, a compelling image or metaphor, a profound idea expressed in a memorable line or two, what John Donne called "the contraction of immensities." My own understanding of the faith has been enriched by the poetry of such people as W. H. Auden, T. S. Eliot, W. B. Yeats, by the great hymns of the church, and by the poetry of the Bible itself, and that also is reflected in these pages.[5] Furthermore, because the wonder of Christmas is often more appropriately sung than spoken, I allow familiar lines of Christmas carols and other hymns to underscore the mystery and meaning of God with us. It has been my experience that to quote a portion of a hymn or carol in a sermon both taps the memory of the congregation and helps us all to sing with renewed attention and appreciation.

As a resource for proclamation, study, and meditation during the Advent-Christmas season, this volume seeks to honor the mystery and to proclaim the meaning of the advent, birth, and epiphany of God in Jesus Christ. Any such intention or attempt presumes upon the mercy of God. Thus, in whole and in each part, this book is prefaced by a silent prayer of confession for the inadequacy of its content and followed by a claim of God's forgiveness for the life of the author.

One

The Encompassing Mystery

In the beginning God created the heavens and the earth.
(Genesis 1:1)

And [God] said . . . "It is done! I am the Alpha and the
Omega, the beginning and the end." *(Revelation 21:6)*

In a well-known lecture series at Cambridge
University in England, the charter of foundation
instructs that each lecturer is to deal with one or more
of the attributes of God. Then, with the delightful
British bent for underscoring the obvious, it adds,
"When these are exhausted" one may go on to some
other subject.[1]

In the same vein: The seminary student approached
the experienced preacher to ask for advice on what to
preach about. The older man was silent for a moment
and then replied, "Preach about God, and preach about
twenty minutes." He meant that the Christian preacher
has numerous opportunities, but one overriding,

inexhaustible theme. Christian preaching grows out of
the mystery of One to whom the psalmist sings:

> O Lord, Thou hast searched me and known me!
> Thou . . . discernest my thoughts from afar.
> Thou . . . art acquainted with all my ways. . . .
> Thou dost beset me behind and before,
>   and layest thy hand upon me.
> Such knowledge is too wonderful for me . . .
>   I cannot attain it.
>
> *Psalm 139:1-6*

We begin not with our understanding of God, but with
God's knowledge of us—not with human wisdom or
religious insight, but with what God has made known
of himself in human history, among human communities, and in the lives of men and women.

This advent of God, this movement of God toward us,
dominates the unfolding drama of the Bible. In the call
and promise to Abraham, it is present in Israel's earliest
historical memory: "Now the Lord said to Abram, 'Go
from your country and your kindred and your father's
house to the land that I will show you. And I will make of
you a great nation . . . and by you all the families of the
earth shall be blessed' " (Genesis 12:1-3).

In the Exodus, God enters into human suffering,
delivers the oppressed, and promises his effective
presence with and for his people. Consider these
possible translations of *Yahweh* in Exodus 3:14:

> I am who I will be.
> I will be there for you.
> He who is indeed with you.

In the life, death, and resurrection of Jesus Christ, God's promised presence comes to full expression. The word is made flesh and dwells among us, full of grace and truth. And the risen Christ, in his farewell promise, claims and secures God's future with us and our future with God: "Lo, I am with you always" (Matthew 28:20).

But God's movement toward us actually begins with the creation of heaven and earth. Even "in the beginning" the promise of Christmas is present. Creation already looks toward God's eternal dwelling with humanity. God's love, God's grace, God's forgiveness are the foundations of the divine intention, not mere afterthoughts. In placing the Genesis account of the creation of heaven and earth at the beginning and the vision of a new heaven and a new earth at the end, the Bible constructs the arena for the advent of God.

> In the beginning God created the heavens and the earth. *(Genesis 1:1)*

> And [God] said . . . "It is done! I am the Alpha and the Omega, the beginning and the end." *(Revelation 21:6)*

Our Advent preparation begins properly with an awareness of the encompassing mystery of God. Into that mystery we fling our prayer: "O come, O come Emmanuel!"

I.

In the beginning, God. . . . That is a confession of faith, or better still, a hymn of praise: "In the beginning

13

God created the heavens and the earth." That is not a scientific theory or physical description of the beginning of the cosmos. We can converse about the universe in scientific terms if we wish. Indeed, we should do so with confidence and gratitude. We know that the universe is millions of years old. Mathematics and astronomy, physics and archaeology help us to discover many of its secrets and perhaps to solve problems connected with its origin and evolution. But we will do well to remember that there is a difference between a *problem*, which can be solved by greater knowledge, and a *mystery*, which is enhanced by knowledge. The proper response to a problem is hard work, study, research, and experimentation. The proper response to mystery is wonder, awe, prayer, and worship.

Consider, for example, the problems of birth defects and fatal illness. Many such problems have been, are being, and will be solved by scientific research and medical skill. But the mystery of life remains and deepens when we contemplate the birth of a child or when we live through the death of a loved one. "The closest I have ever felt to God," says my father-in-law, "was when my children were born and I held them in my arms, and when my father died." Most of us remember the moon landing. That event represents a solution to the problem of space travel. But do you also remember the picture of earth taken from the moon— the globe on which we live and die and solve our problems, suspended there in the vastness of space?

That only sharpened the mystery and wonder of our world. Paul Tillich used to tell with delight of a question his six-year-old daughter asked. "Why are trees not not?" (Why are there trees anyway?) A botanist may some day know all there is to know about how trees are there, but no botanist as a botanist will ever know why there is a tree anyway. "Why are trees not not?" We recall the psalmist's words: "Out of the mouths of babes . . . thou hast rebuked the mighty" (Psalm 8:2 NEB).

However many problems we may solve, what can we know about our world that is more important than the following words?

> In the beginning God created the heavens and the earth. The earth was without form and void, and darkness was upon the face of the deep; and the Spirit of God was moving over the face of the waters. And God said, "Let there be light"; and there was light. . . . Then God said, "Let us make man in our image, after our likeness . . ." So God created man in his own image, in the image of God he created him; male and female he created them. *(Genesis 1:1-3, 26a, 27)*

That is truth which can only be confessed and sung, not explained. The biblical doctrine of creation is calculated neither to explain the origin of the world at some datable moment in the cosmic past nor to describe literally the beginning of time. The Genesis picture of God's calling the world into being out of nothing is not a scientific statement about a historical event, but a theological confession about the deepest meaning of existence. The Hebrew word translated here "to create" is a verb that is used only with God as its subject. The implication of that verb choice is that here we have truth far beyond our ability to explain it, but not beyond our capacity to confess. It is truth beyond human conceiving, but not beyond our trust. John S. Whale wrote: "The doctrine of creation out of nothing is not a cosmological theory, but an expression of our adoring sense of the transcendent majesty of God, and our utter dependence upon Him."[2]

In the same vein, but more colorfully, G. K. Chesterton once commented that the sun does not rise "merely as the result of the earth's motion. It rises because God says 'Get up.' "[3] Nor does the theory of the evolution of the human race from lower mammalian life, which biological evidence seems to support, affect for one moment the truth that human beings have their origin and essential being in a word addressed to them by God, their Creator.

We talk about putting God first. Do you really think it matters for a moment where we put God? God is first! By beginning with this hymn of praise to God, who called the world into being, the Bible makes us this proposition: It will introduce us to the wisdom and the will, to the grace and the love, to the power and the truth—the Word back of all created things, undergirding all knowledge, encompassing all of time. We may believe it or not; that is our business. Either way: "In the beginning God. . . ." And the stage is set.

II.

In the beginning, God. . . . Genesis 1 sets the stage. So also, God in the end; Revelation 21 completes the scene. This is the message of the strange and mysterious book of Revelation. In the end, God . . . , with all the courage and comfort and joy that implies.

The scene in Revelation is appropriately cosmic. The whole created order fills this vision of a new heaven and a new earth, conforming in every way to God's purpose and dominated in every way by God's presence. It is a glad scene. Individuals are reconciled to God, and nature and history are redeemed as well. The message of Revelation is gospel, not gloom! The Bible does not end with despair, but with a song of God's victory and our hope:

The Lord God omnipotent reigneth! *(Revelation 19:6 KJV)*

Behold, the dwelling of God is with men. He will dwell with them, and they shall be his people, and God himself will be with them. *(Revelation 21:3)*

If we are to hear Revelation's message of hope and triumph, it is important to avoid a literal understanding of its highly symbolic language and imagery. For example, Revelation does not give us a blueprint for the end of time. To use this book to determine when and how the world will end or to identify who are the saved and how many or to equate some contemporary political figure with the Antichrist is to misuse it. To

17

argue from Revelation to an exclusive view of humanity's relation to God as though our way, or some particular way, were the only way into his heart at the end of history is to miss its meaning altogether. Rather we should let the artistry and poetry and music of this book have its way with us until the sheer, shimmering grace of it melts away any cruel exclusiveness we cling to. Consider, for example, the wonderful imagery in that final vision of the heavenly city in chapters 21 and 22. The judgment of God is real, but we have moved here through and beyond judgment to redemption. There are twelve gates, we are told, and then: "The city has no need of sun or moon to shine upon it, for the glory of God is its light, and its lamp is the Lamb [Christ]. By its light shall the nations walk . . . and its gates shall never be shut by day—and there shall be no night there" (Revelation 21:23-25).

What a telling way to show that the gates of God's mercy are ever open! The gates of the city are never closed while it is day, and there is no night! Jesus warned the disciples about wanting to know the "times or seasons which the Father has fixed by his own authority" (Acts 1:7). The consummation of history, its judgment and redemption, is hidden. But like our own lives, it is "hidden with Christ in God" (Colossians 3:3 NEB) from beginning to end.

We who would proclaim the triumph of grace in this marvelous book at the end of the Bible shall ever be in the debt of the composer, George F. Handel, who set it to music in the "Hallelujah Chorus" of the *Messiah*. Its text consists of verses from Revelation:

Allelujah: for the Lord God omnipotent reigneth. . . . The
kingdoms of this world are become the kingdoms of our Lord,
and of his Christ; and he shall reign for ever and ever. . . .
King of Kings, and Lord of Lords. (*Revelation 19:6; 11:15; 19:16
KJV*)

III.

In the beginning, God. In the end, God. And in
between, Emmanuel—God with us in the very bundle
of living.

Any proclamation and interpretation of this gospel
must acknowledge that Emmanuel has to do not only
with Christmas and comfort, but also with a cross.
Emmanuel means "God with us" not merely, or even
primarily, to shield us from the dark side of life, but to
be with us and to go with us through the valley of the
shadow, whether of death or despair, suffering or
tragedy. We cannot knit Genesis and Revelation and
Jesus into a neat little creed and then, using it for a
security blanket, withdraw, leaving God's world to
God. We cannot leave to others the doing of what really
needs to be done. This vision of God in the beginning,
God in the end, and God with us in Jesus Christ is a call
to, not a substitute for, obedient action and faithful
living in the world. Said Paul Scherer:

If this vision [we] have of God does not move and drive and
pull and tug and wrench and twist and hold and stride and
walk off grimly after Him, it is nothing. We stultify it when we

19

use it as a solace and no more. We prostitute it when we hitch
it to some private little enterprise against headaches. . . . This
is to take the power of God that swings the stars in their orbits
and ask it to do nothing but the household chores.[4]

The gospel of Emmanuel is something other than a
technique for making things easy. "The God who is
primarily a helper toward the attainment of human
wishes," said H. Richard Niebuhr, "is not the being to
whom Christ said, 'Thy will, not mine, be done.' "[5]
There is a cross at the heart of this faith of ours, and a cry
of anguish: "My God, my God, why hast thou forsaken
me?" (Mark 15:34) and a whispered prayer of utter
trust: "Father, into thy hands I commit my spirit!"
(Luke 23:46).

In the story of David, Abigail, who later becomes
David's second wife, says to him: "If men rise up to
pursue you and to seek your life, the life of my lord shall
be bound in the bundle of the living in the care of the
Lord your God" (I Samuel 25:29). Something like that is
the assurance we are meant to draw from the way the
Bible begins and ends. The encompassing mystery
graciously upholds and sustains us. In our time, faith,
hope, and love are beset by pain and violence. To live
by faith may not mean less pain or less distress; the way
of faith is not a detour around adversity. Indeed, there
are circumstances in which faith seems only to sustain
us, to help us endure. Sometimes we can do no more
than cling to the faith of others. Sometimes the faith of
the church, locally and historically, has to bear us along
in our doubt and disability. We are like the paralytic
brought to Jesus by his friends. "There are times when I

just cannot say the creed," said one of my parishioners. "I'll say it for you until you can say it again," I replied. "Whether or not you were aware of it, there have been times when you have had to say it for me; and I shall probably need you to do so again in the future. That is one thing we mean by 'the communion of saints.' That is one reason we are given to one another in the church." Devout women and men across the ages until now can testify to that. There are times when we have to refrain from saying to one another, "Keep the faith!" in order to say a more appropriate word: "Let the faith keep you!"

Furthermore, our calling as Christian people is to live against evil, to oppose the woes that afflict humanity and to stand against their human causes. We cannot responsibly leave misery unalleviated. We must not leave social reform to the angry and the selfish, even the angry and the selfish within the Christian community, who are all of us some of the time and some of us most of the time. We dare not stand aloof from what Keats called, "the giant agony of the world"; to do so is a kind of practical atheism in the face of the good news of a God who created the heavens and the earth, who so loved the world that he gave his only Son, and who shall reign as King of kings and Lord of lords forever and ever. This has always been the courage in which Christians have faced up to evil, and faced it down—the assurance that "your life shall be bound in the bundle of the living in the care of the Lord your God" (I Samuel 25:29).

IV.

In the beginning, God; in the end, God. Like the anthems of two great choirs, the Genesis hymn of creation and the crescendo of the "Hallelujah Chorus" enfold the cosmos and every creature, the whole of time and every life, in the encompassing mystery of God.

Our preparation for the advent of God begins in silence as we await a word from beyond ourselves, from within the mystery.

> Let all mortal flesh keep silence,
> And with fear and trembling stand;
> Ponder nothing earthly minded,
> For with blessing in his hand,
> Christ our God to earth descendeth,
> Our full homage to demand.

> ("Let All Mortal Flesh Keep Silence")

Out of the encompassing mystery, God comes to us at Christmas—and not as a stranger. As the fourth Gospel puts it, he comes unto his own, and even if "his own" will not receive him, as is so often the case with us, the fact remains that we are his. We are his own from the outset. We have no past existence in which we might have been created and prepared for something other than the grace of God. God claimed us "before the foundation of the world" (Ephesians 1:4). We may doubt, deny, or renounce God's claim, but God will never relinquish his claim. We have no future existence in which we might be destined for something other than God's judging and redeeming love.[6]

We conclude with a visual illustration. There at the very center of things, like a circle drawn in the middle of life, is God, whose gracious will, irrevocable decision, and invincible purpose is to be Emmanuel, God with us. Around that core, from the same center in God, is drawn another circle. It is the circle of God's judgments; so that nobody is ever able to break out of the first without running headlong into the second. It is possible to stop there if one so chooses. But beyond is a third circle, drawn more widely still: the circle of God's grace—his first word and his last, which is the origin and destiny of all existence and of every life. The arcs of that last circle, like two great loving arms, gather the world into an eternal embrace.[7]

Two

The Mystery Set Forth in Christ

God said to Moses, "I am who I will be." And he said, "Say this to the people of Israel, 'I will be there for you' . . . this is my name for ever." *(Exodus 3:14-15, author's translation)*

For [God] has made known to us in all wisdom and insight the mystery of his will, according to his purpose which he set forth in Christ. *(Ephesians 1:9)*

A chess master, observing a particular move in a game he had been watching, said to his companion, "That's it!" He meant that the move had been made that would ultimately determine the outcome of the game. The players themselves may have been unaware of it. The other observers may not have noticed anything of significance having taken place. There would surely be numerous other moves made in the match. The other player might stave off defeat for some time yet by an offensive play here or a defensive maneuver there. But the master player knew he had seen the decisive move, and from that moment of insight, he watched the match, confident of its outcome.

The above texts from Exodus and Ephesians speak of revelation—that event in which the purpose of life breaks in on us from beyond, that particular part of our history which gives meaning to the whole of it, that moment of mystery and clarity in which, however briefly, we catch a glimpse of the very mind and heart of God and cry out, "That's it!" T. S. Eliot spoke of revelation as one moment that gives meaning to the whole of time, an event by which time is literally "made":

> A moment in time but time was made through that moment:
> for without the meaning, there is no time, and that moment
> of time gave the meaning.[1]

For the Christian community, that special event, that moment in time, is Jesus Christ. "Revelation means for us that part of our inner history which illuminates the rest of it and which is itself intelligible," wrote H. Richard Niebuhr. "The special occasion to which we appeal in the Christian church is called Jesus Christ, in whom we see the righteousness of God, his power and wisdom. But from that special occasion we also derive the concepts which make possible the elucidation of all events in our history."[2] In Jesus Christ, Christians confess, God has opened his mind and heart to us. Through him God "has made known to us in all wisdom and insight the mystery of his will." Paul echoed this in other ways:

For it is the God who said, "Let light shine out of darkness," who has shone in our hearts to give the light of the knowledge of the glory of God in the face of Christ. *(II Corinthians 4:6)*

For in him all the fulness of God was pleased to dwell. *(Colossians 1:19)*

John said the same thing in his own way:

"In the beginning was the Word, and the Word was with God, and the Word was God. . . . And the Word became flesh and dwelt among us." *(John 1:1, 14)*

For the author of Hebrews, "[Christ] reflects the glory of God and bears the very stamp of his nature" (Hebrews 1:3). Martin Luther called him "the mirror of the fatherly heart of God." The Scottish theologian P. T. Forsyth said that Jesus Christ is "God's account of Himself."

For [God] has made known to us in all wisdom and insight the mystery of his will, according to his purpose which he set forth in Christ as a plan for the fulness of time, to unite all things in him, things in heaven and things on earth. *(Ephesians 1:9-10)*

Our subject, then, is revelation—the mystery set forth in Christ.

I.

To begin, we acknowledge that revelation involves both giving and withholding. Revelation is the setting forth of a *mystery* that remains and continues around us. In the classic biblical text on revelation, Exodus 3, God grants Moses' request and makes his name known. Yahweh, however, is a mysterious name. It does not define God in such a way that Moses or Israel or anyone else can henceforth control, manage, or make God accessible on their own terms. God withholds himself from human control even as he gives his name, which is a mysterious promise to be faithfully and effectively present with and for his people on his own terms: "I am who I will be"; "I will be there for you"; "He who is indeed with you."

God moves in on us, as it were, out of the encompassing mystery, from the pages of the Bible, in the person of Jesus Christ. Revelation comes as an encounter, an address. In that moment we know that we are contingent, dependent, obligated, responsible, and accountable. Revelation lets us know that we are known, from beginning to end, by Another who meets us there along the way of life. Revelation means knowing that even as we presume to sit in judgment on others, there is One who, in a much profounder sense, judges us. Revelation means becoming aware that even as we put value on people and things, there is One who values us all beyond our wildest dreams. Revelation means that even as we think about God and seek God and claim to know God, we are ourselves, long beforehand, thought, found, and known of God. We sense, in some moments at least, that if we are ever to understand the meaning of life within the parentheses of birth and death that bracket human existence, we must know the nature of the mystery outside the parentheses. What or Who is this mysterious Knower, Searcher, Thinker, Valuer, Judge that addresses us? Is this One an impersonal force? A fantasy? A "Thou"?

The psalmist encounters God as a mysterious "Thou":

> O Lord, thou hast searched me and known me!
> Thou knowest when I sit down and when I rise up;
>   thou discernest my thoughts from afar. . . .
> Whither shall I go from thy Spirit?
>   Or whither shall I flee from thy presence?
> If I ascend to heaven, thou art there!
>   If I make my bed in Sheol, thou art there!
> If I take the wings of the morning
>   and dwell in the uttermost parts of the sea,
> even there thy hand shall lead me,
>   and thy right hand shall hold me.
>
> *Psalm 139:1-2, 7-10*

Christian faith makes the staggering claim that the mystery that encompasses and addresses us "became flesh and dwelt among us" in person. The mystery has a name and a face (cf. II Corinthians 4:6), and is "full of grace and truth."

> For [God] has made known to us in all wisdom and insight the mystery of his will, according to his purpose which he set forth in Christ as a plan for the fulness of time, to unite all things in heaven and things on earth. *(Ephesians 1:9-10)*

This is no claim that the mystery has been solved or that it is exhausted; only that in Jesus Christ we have to do with a God who is and remains *mysterious*. And with Paul we confess, "Now I know in part; then I shall understand fully, even as I have been fully understood" (I Corinthians 13:12).

II.

God is mysterious. God is also *gracious*. God has set forth the mystery of his will. Of his own free decision, without ceasing for a moment to be veiled in mystery, God moved toward us, accommodated himself to us, and took his place beside us and among us.

As we have seen, to Moses God sets himself forth as the faithful One who will accompany and provide for his people. This setting forth continues as God's story with humanity unfolds.

God is the compassionate One who sustains and upholds us:

Hearken to me, O house of Jacob,
    all the remnant of the house of Israel,
who have been borne by me from your birth,
    carried from the womb;
even to your old age I am He,
    and to gray hairs I will carry you.
I have made, and I will bear;
    I will carry and will save.

Isaiah 46:3-4

[The Lord] heals the brokenhearted,
    and binds up their wounds. . . .
The Lord lifts up the downtrodden.

Psalm 147:3, 6

God is the merciful One who meets us in our sin and disobedience as Judge and Redeemer:

> For a brief moment I forsook you,
>   but with great compassion I will
>   gather you.
> In overflowing wrath for a moment
>   I hid my face from you,
> but with everlasting love I will have
>   compassion on you,
>   says the Lord, your Redeemer. . . .
>
> For the mountains may depart
>   and the hills be removed,
> but my steadfast love shall not
>   depart from you,
>   and my covenant of peace shall
>   not be removed,
>   says the Lord, who has
>   compassion on you.

Isaiah 54:7-8, 10

Because God has opened his heart and mind to us, we dare to live with a basic confidence in and about the world. We may understand, and even sympathize with, but we are not convinced by the pessimism of Betrand Russell who wrote that

> we see, surrounding the narrow raft illumined by the flickering light of human comradeship, the dark ocean on whose rolling waves we toss for a brief hour; from the great night without, a chill blast breaks in upon our refuge; all the loneliness of humanity amid hostile forces is concentrated upon the individual soul, which must struggle alone, with what of courage it can command, against the whole weight of a universe that cares nothing for its hopes and fears.[3]

Instead, we speak of that grace which is the presupposition of creation, and we confess that life is a gift and the Giver can be trusted. "The eternal God is thy refuge, and underneath are the everlasting arms" (Deuteronomy 33:27 KJV). Moreover, in that confidence we begin to see around, among, and within us signs of guilt overcome by grace, greed overcome by gratitude, self-concern overcome by generosity, hostility overcome by gentleness, arrogance overcome by graciousness, and narrow-mindedness overcome by great-heartedness.

Someone spoke words such as these in a presentation to a group of theologians, whereupon one of them said wistfully, "I wish I could be sure." As those who struggle honestly and faithfully to proclaim this gospel in and to a hurting world, we can both appreciate the longing and identify with it. Indeed, how can we be certain that the mystery is gracious? We need someone who is of the mystery, yet has lived and died with us. This brings us to the final word about the mystery set forth in Christ.

III.

God is mysterious. God is gracious. God is *personal*. God has set forth the mystery of his will and purpose in Jesus Christ. At its deepest level, God's revelation of himself takes the form of a person. In a child born of woman, swaddled in linen bands, and laid in a manger, the eternal mystery of origin, purpose, and destiny has come to us in person.

31

The Word became flesh and dwelt among us, full of grace and
truth. *(John 1:14)*

In many and various ways God spoke of old to our fathers by
the prophets; but in these last days he has spoken to us by a
Son. *(Hebrews 1:1-2)*

We are not talking about something divine, something
akin to God or like God. No, we are talking about God's
setting forth himself in a human life—the scandal of
particularity. So great is God's love for us that he refuses
to be anything less than God, himself, with us in person.

This is why we have all the to-do about Christmas.
Christmas means revelation: the sovereign, gracious,
merciful, reconciling, redeeming event in which all other
events are given meaning. "For God has made known to
us in all wisdom and insight the mystery of his will
according to his purpose which he set forth in Christ as a
plan for the fullness of time, to unite all things in him,
things in heaven and things on earth" (Ephesians 1:9-10).

Revelation, Paul Scherer reminds us, "is not a record,
it is a gift. It is not a philosophy built up from underneath;
it is the weight and the pressure itself of a life beyond our
own, of Whom, and through Whom, and to Whom are
all things."[4] In the fullness of time, from deep within the
mystery of his being, God sets forth in grace and love,
and Christ is born. "That's it!" we say. That One is God
with us: the *mystery* that compels our reverent silence;
the *grace* that bids us, "Rejoice! Rejoice! Emmanuel has
come to thee!"; the *love* so personal as to call us sons and
daughters and bid us call him Abba, Father! If someone
says to us, "That's just too good to be true!" we answer,
"No, my friend, that's too good *not* to be true!"

Three

The Birth of God

Behold, a virgin shall conceive and bear a son, and his name shall be called Emmanuel (which means, God with us). *(Matthew 1:23)*

And Mary said, "Behold, I am the handmaid of the Lord; let it be to me according to your word." *(Luke 1:38)*

In a diverse little collection of writings entitled *Fragments Grave and Gay*, Karl Barth tells of coming across a six-hundred-year-old contract for the sale of a house. Written in solemn language required in such matters even in those days, it was dated as follows: "Given at Basle on the first Monday after Pope St. Urban's day in the one thousand three hundred seventy first year counting from the birth of God."[1]

"Counting from the birth of God." Even where money and property, trading and trafficking, were concerned, said Barth, the people of the Middle Ages knew more than we about the secret of their age, their history and their life.

33

Christmas is where everything, and everyone, "counts" from. Christmas is where politics and economics derive their meaning and purpose, whoever is issuing the decrees or revising the tax laws. Christmas is where history has laid bare its hidden foundation and its hidden goal in One whose name is Emmanuel. At Christmas the cosmos sings the "Gloria in Excelsis" in response to the Creator's "Let there be . . . born unto you a Savior." Christmas is where "the hopes and fears of all the years" are met, including the hopes and fears of this year late in the twentieth century, "counting from the birth of God."

I.

Of course, to speak of Christmas in terms of the birth of God is to plunge into the deepest mystery of life. One thinks immediately of John's *mysterium tremendum:* "In the beginning was the Word, and the Word was with God, and the Word was God. . . . And the Word became flesh and dwelt among us" (John 1:1, 14). Matthew and Luke, for all the tenderness and familiarity of their birth stories, are equally aware of the mystery. In the birth of One whose name shall be called Emmanuel, Matthew sees the fulfillment of the mysterious promise that moves and drives, carries and keeps, judges and sustains the people of God across the pages of history: "I am who I will be . . . I will be with you . . . I will be there for you." That same promise closes Matthew's Gospel in the Great Commission of

34

the risen Christ: "Lo, I am with you always." And mystery pulsates in Luke's lovely story. Our favorite carols have set it to music for us: the silent night, while shepherds watched their flocks and heaven and nature sang around the little town, lying still for the birth of One who, like the universe he will redeem, has his origin in the Word of God.

It happened, say Matthew and Luke, at a particular time, in a particular place, in connection with a particular mother: "In the days of Herod the king," "when Quirinius was governor of Syria," "in Bethlehem," "of Mary." In many ways it was no different from any other birth on that day. According to Luke, a census was being taken across the empire. Perhaps Jesus got counted along with everybody else. Like many others, he was born to parents of lowly estate and humble means. He was wrapped in cloth against the chill, held in his mother's arms, and fed at her breast.

Yet, with the astonishing claim that this One was conceived by the Holy Spirit and born of Mary, a virgin, the whole business fairly shimmers with the mystery of the Word made flesh. In these stories of Matthew and Luke, the virgin birth is a sign, a confession, a way of expressing the deep mystery of Christmas as the birth of God. It is not an explanation or a solution. It is certainly not a proof, as if Christmas were answerable to our science or reason or logic. Indeed, over against any explanation we would offer for this thing that has come to pass, the virgin birth stands as "the guard at the door to the mystery of Christmas" (Karl Barth).

II.

The guard is posted in the Apostles' Creed—an Advent sentry: "Conceived by the Holy Ghost, born of the virgin Mary."

In my own ministry, I have found this to be one of the places in the confession of the church at which many people take offense. For some people, both inside and outside the church, this is nothing more than "primitive mythology." For others, it is nothing less than the acid test of Christian orthodoxy. Still others simply repeat the words uncomfortably when the Creed is recited, or, with equal discomfort, remain silent altogether.

Furthermore, when questions come about the virgin birth, they all too often are anxious and defensive questions: "Must I believe this?" "Am I expected to accept that?" There was once a dear lady on the pulpit committee of a church for whom this was the only real question of any candidate. "I have just one question," she would ask defiantly. "Do you believe in the virgin birth?"

But the anxious, defensive, defiant questions are the wrong ones. A person can certainly confess Jesus Christ as Lord and Savior, and even as the Son of God, without affirming the virgin birth as a biological statement. Before we make this doctrine the cornerstone of orthodoxy, we might consider that the earliest Christian preaching we know about did not mention it. Before the New Testament canon was compiled, many Christians in the early church never had access to the Gospels of Luke or Matthew; they perhaps knew Mark or John, if indeed they read any Gospel. Paul does not seem to have thought this an essential of Christian faith; he never mentions it. Moreover, neither the validity of Old Testament prophecy nor the substance of Old Testament hope, neither the proclamation of the early church nor the truth of the Creed, depends upon the virgin birth as a demonstrable biological fact.

But that is not where the matter ends. That is where the matter begins! The purpose of the birth stories in Matthew and Luke is not to set or to solve a biological problem, but to introduce us to and to invite us to the deepest mystery of God's grace. Here Matthew and Luke set before us not an explanation, calculated to make Christmas manageable for us, not an argument to win our assent, not a proof to close the case, but the story of a miracle—an event of which only God could be the subject—with which you and I must wrestle for the rest of this chapter and for the rest of this season and for the rest of our lives.

What is a miracle, after all? It is not fundamentaly some rending of the natural order. It is not finally some supernatural twisting of the laws of nature. At its deepest level, a miracle is an event, any event, in which the transcendent breaks through to us with a vision of meaning and purpose, truth and value, identity and destiny, judgment and mercy—with a vision of God. A miracle is an event that lets us see, but not solve, the transcendent mystery that encompasses our life.

The church knew well what it was doing when it posted the virgin birth on guard at the doorway to Christmas. Perhaps we consider ourselves too sophisticated for such "sentimental mythology." Perhaps we have more important things to attend to in our resolve to "make Christmas more meaningful" this year. So, with our no-nonsense minds and well intentioned plans, we rush up to the threshold of Christmas where this strange guard meets us with a word of challenge and welcome, of judgment and grace: "Conceived by the Holy Ghost, born of the virgin Mary."

III.

"Born of the virgin Mary" means born as no one else was born, born in a way that cannot be described, much less explained, biologically. The virgin birth is a judgment upon humanity. What distinguishes the birth of Christ and marks it as God's mystery is what it lacks, namely, human self-assertion, human achievement, and human initiative. As we hurry past it year after year, the virgin birth reminds us that we cannot create Christmas. We cannot "keep" Christmas as if it were ours to control. We cannot "make it meaningful" this year or any year. We cannot "put Christ back in Christmas" because we did not put Christ there to begin with. We can only receive Christmas, receive the Christ as a gift from the hand and heart of God.

As always, beyond the judgment there is grace. "Born of the virgin Mary" also means that Jesus Christ is really born—of a woman. The mystery of Christmas is not an event in the loneliness of God, but a gracious event between God and humanity. In Mary, humanity is involved, but only in Mary as the Virgin Mary, only as one who receives, who is ready, who lets something be done to and with herself. "And Mary said, 'Behold, I am the handmaid of the Lord; let it be to me according to your word' " (Luke 1:38). Mary is humanity waiting in readiness for God.

IV.

Again the guard speaks: "Conceived by the Holy Ghost." Once more, it is a word of judgment and grace. "Conceived by the Holy Ghost" is a renunciation of any biological understanding of Christmas. It is a way of saying that to desire or propose an explanation of Christmas from biology or physics is to deny the mystery and to make Christmas manageable, or at least to try to make it so. Sex is excluded from the mystery of Christmas not because sex is sinful, but because no event of human initiative can give birth to God.

But again, the grace sounds more forcefully even than the judgment here: "Conceived by the Holy Ghost." What we cannot conceive or accomplish, God can and does. "Conceived by the Holy Ghost" means, for *Matthew*, that God has come through on the promise. God (and not some human agent) is the author of the mystery of Christmas in the birth of Emmanuel.

"Conceived by the Holy Ghost" means, for *Luke*, that God has said: "Let there be . . . unto you a Savior who is Christ the Lord." Mary answers, "Behold I am the handmaid of the Lord; let it be to me according to your word." At this point, Luke would have us think of

Genesis—God's calling the world into being out of nothing, the calling of order out of cosmic chaos, light out of thick darkness, purpose and promise out of Babel's confusion, birth and blessing out of Sarah's barrenness, and hope out of despair. In the story of the annunciation to Mary, Luke would have us think of the God who speaks "and it [is] so." The ancient theologian, John of Damascus, is essentially right when he identifies Mary's *ear* as the bodily organ of the miraculous conception of Christ.

> And Mary said, "Behold, I am the handmaid of the Lord; let it be to me according to your word."

V.

"Conceived by the Holy Ghost, born of the virgin Mary." Thus our Advent sentry reminds us from his credal post that Christmas is an event without comparison. God's coming to us, as the name Emmanuel suggests, takes place without any human initiative and without effectual cause. There is no "why," no "whence," no "how." God simply makes a beginning with himself. From Mary we learn of the only way a human being can have a part in it. "Behold I am the handmaid of the Lord. Let it be to me according to your word."

But is it really necessary to signify the mystery of Christmas, God with us, by making the statement that Jesus was conceived by the Holy Ghost and born of the virgin Mary? It still has that dogmatic ring against which modern men and women react with strong suspicion, if not irritation. "Must I believe in that to be a Christian?" "Can I not do without that?" But it is here that we who preach and teach the Christmas gospel have a particular pastoral opportunity to say that it is not a question of doing anything. One is not a Christian because one does, thinks, believes, experiences, or says something. Certainly one is not a Christian, and does not become one, just by repeating the Creed. Christmas is not about our finding or confessing God, but about God's drawing near to us.

On God's initiative and by his grace, we are drawn into the circle of Christian faith as the mystery of Christmas takes hold of us and as the words and stories stir us and as the carols thrill us and as the silence whispers to our deepest hopes and as the steadfast love of God in Christ holds on to us for dear life and as the sheer grace of it all calls us to trust and obey. Then, even with halting words and imperfect signs, we can repeat what we have heard: that Christmas does affect "modern man" in exactly the same manner it affected ancient man and woman and medieval man and woman and as it will affect men and women in the year three thousand "counting from the birth of God."

Is there anything better you or I can do as Christmas comes than to go forth into the season with this confession?

Do not be afraid . . . you have found favor with God . . .

To you is born this day in the city of David a Savior, who is Christ the Lord . . . *(Luke 1:30; 2:11)*

The Birth of God

And his name shall be called Emmanuel . . . God with us.
(Matthew 1:23)

With this confession, questions become relevant that
are quite different from the anxious question, "Must I
believe in that?" There is no "must" about it. It is a
matter of being free to trust, not because we must, but
because we *may*. Or more profoundly, because now we
and all things "count" from the birth of God, we can do
little else but join hearts and voices with those in the
Christmas drama.

The Magi in homage:

"Where is he who has been born. . . ?
For we have seen his star . . . and have come to worship
him." *(Matthew 2:2)*

The shepherds in adoration:

"Let us go over to Bethlehem and see this thing that has
happened." *(Luke 2:15)*

The angels in praise:

"Glory to God in the highest, and on earth peace." *(Luke 2:14)*

And Mary in faith:

"Let it be to me according to your word." *(Luke 1:38)*

Six

The Keeper of Your Life

The Lord is your keeper . . . he will keep your life. *(Psalm 121:5a, 7b)*

For from him and through him and to him are all things. *(Romans 11:36a)*

His steadfast love endures for ever. *(Psalm 136:1b)*

All five candles of the Advent wreath on our breakfast table are burning. The story has been read and reread; the children have known it by heart for better than a decade. They seem never to tire of hearing it one more time. They want no monkeying about with it either, whether it is humorist Garrison Keillor talking about the assistant wise man, the associate wise man, and the chairman of the Wisdom Department who came from an eastern university, or their own father saying that the sheep's names are Surely, Goodness, and Mercy. As in Advents past, they have rearranged the figures around the crêche in the den dozens of times. Entering into the drama, and handling the mystery enhances the wonder and joy somehow. Over recent days, we have sung the carols; we have celebrated the Sacrament; we have received the Gift; and we have exchanged gifts. Soon, however, we begin to feel Christmas slipping away. The children are as aware of the well-known "letdown" as they are sensitive to the proper pace and dramatic movement of Advent. "Christmas is over, definitely over," they announce with a mixture of resignation and regret as no later than New Years' Eve the crêche is put away, the Advent wreath is dismantled, and the tree is taken down. The celebration is soon muted in the return to daily routine, to business as usual.

Since most of us, for whatever reasons, are unable to keep the Christmas mood of wonder and mystery, or to "repeat the sounding joy" beyond about December 28, perhaps these "twelve days of Christmas" are a good time to remember that the One born of Mary and laid in a manger is the One who keeps us. Furthermore, since these days bring the beginning of another new year, we might consider how the Christmas gospel interprets the providence of God, in whose hands are our times—all our days and years.

I.

Psalm 121 speaks of God as the keeper of life:

> The Lord is your keeper. . . .
> The Lord will keep you from all evil;
>   he will keep your life.

The Birth of God

The Lord will keep
   your going out and your coming in
   from this time forth and for evermore.

(Psalm 121:5a, 5-8)

Underlying this song is the conviction that reverberates in the great chorus of Psalm 136: "for his steadfast love endures for ever." Again and again the words are repeated, like the pulse of eternity surging through life: "His steadfast love endures for ever." The steadfast love of God—the presupposition of creation, the foundation of the cosmos, the well spring of faith and worship, the purpose in and over history, the origin and destiny of human existence and of each and every life. Thus do the psalms sound the depths and probe the limits and reach to the very heart of biblical faith: God, whose steadfast love endures forever, is the keeper of your life.

The New Testament gospel does not differ from that. To the Athenians, Paul declares that all people live and move and have their being in this God of steadfast love, who created the cosmos and the human family, who provides for the world and its inhabitants, and whose love was given its most complete expression in the life, death, and resurrection of Jesus Christ, "the man of God's own choosing," in whom the complete being of God came to dwell (cf. Acts 17:31; Colossians 1:19).

To God's steadfast love, the New Testament compares "the grace of the Lord Jesus Christ." Grace is God's free, unfaltering love of the universe; God's free, unmerited love of humanity; God's loyal and persistent love for each and everyone of us, in which we are preserved, accompanied, and held.

Any proper understanding of God's presence and providence must rest firmly on these parallel foundation stones of faith: the steadfast love of God and the grace of the Lord Jesus Christ. They remind us that we are not on our own in this life. Rather, from beginning to end, we are upheld by a mystery we cannot see, sustained by a power we cannot control, challenged by a righteousness we cannot attain, and redeemed by a mercy we cannot imagine. They express, in all simplicity and profundity, the heart, the mind, and the will of him who keeps our going out and our coming in "from this time forth and for evermore."

II.

Given the "firm foundation" of God's steadfast love and the grace of the Lord Jesus Christ, which "is laid for our faith," we now, in faith, venture a further word for the new year about the care of this God who keeps our life and in whom we live and move and have our being. Paul's cry of exultation at the end of the eleventh chapter of Romans acknowledges both the mystery of the Incarnation and our hope for years to come:

O the depth of the riches and wisdom and knowledge of God! How unsearchable are his judgments and how inscrutable his ways! . . . For from him and through him and to him are all things. To him be glory for ever. *(Romans 11:33, 36)*

This means, first of all, that God keeps your life eternally, not just occasionally. The steadfast love of God is from everlasting to everlasting. Paul's exclamation: "for from him . . . are all things!" does not simply look back to the act of creation, but points to God's continuously preserving his creatures and his world.

The psalms sing of God's keeping creation. He numbers and names the stars (Psalm 147:4). He shelters the birds (Psalm 84:3; cf. Matthew 6:26). He feeds the wild animals (Psalm 104:27-28). He protects and preserves human beings (Psalm 36:7; 73:23-24).

That same faith in God's providential care is delightfully and with great insight expressed in the late Marc Connelly's biblical drama, *The Green Pastures*. In one scene God looks at his world and says that "it is a good earth; I ought to have somebody to enjoy it." Then God calls Gabriel and tells him that he (God) is "going down dere. . . . I want you to be my working boss yere while I'm gone." There follows a marvelous expression of the majestic power and tender care of God, who says to Gabriel as he leaves: "You know dat matter of dem two stars? . . . Git dat fixed up!" And then, recalling Jesus' own example of the Father's infinite capacity for caring: "You know dat sparrow dat fell a little while ago? Tend to dat, too."[1] One could read volumes of commentary and theology, to great advantage, and still not find a more poignant statement of providence.

When sparrows do fall—those we love or ourselves—in such times, the Bible would have us know that the faithfulness of God with his creation and his children is an eternal faithfulness. God's care does not

end when one's life ends. The Bible never denies that
death is real, but it insists that God's faithfulness
continues in, through, and beyond death. We die, but
we do not die into nothingness; we die into God, and,
therefore, we are eternally preserved. "Your life is
hidden with Christ in God" (Colossians 3:3). This
means, suggests Karl Barth, that no one will ever perish
apart from God, and nothing will escape God—nothing. No event in a remote corner of creation,

> no moment of human life; no thinking thought; no word
> spoken . . . no suffering or joy; no sincerity or lie; no secret
> event in heaven or too well-known event on earth; no ray of
> sunlight; no note which has ever sounded; no colour which
> has ever been revealed, possibly in the darkness of oceanic
> depths where the eye of man has never perceived it; no
> wing-beat of the day-fly in far-flung epochs of geological time.
> Everything [and everyone] will be present to [God] exactly as
> it was or is or will be, in all its reality, in the whole temporal
> course of its activity, in its strength or weakness, in its majesty
> or meanness. [God] will not allow anything to perish, but will
> hold it in the hollow of His hand as He has always done, and
> does, and will do. He will not be alone in eternity, but with the
> creature. He will allow [us] to partake of His own eternal life.[2]

A poem by Arthur Hugh Clough entitled "With
Whom Is No Shadow of Variableness" speaks of God's
constancy as the keeper of life:

> It fortifies my soul to know
> That, though I perish, Truth is so;
> That howsoe'er I stray or range,
> Whate'er I do, Thou dost not change.
> I steadier step when I recall
> That, if I slip, Thou dost not fall.

God keeps you eternally, "for *from* him are all things."

III.

The second part of Paul's exclamation means that God keeps our lives presently, not just on some grand scale, uninvolved in our living and dying day by day, but here and now in the bundle of activity and relationships that is your life and my life. "For . . . through him . . . are all things!" refers less to God as an abstract First Cause than to the mysterious, transcendent Creator who is also God with us. Paul Gerhardt wrote the hymn "Commit Thou All Thy Griefs":

Who points the stars their course,
Whom winds and seas obey,
He shall direct thy wandering feet,
He shall prepare thy way.

In the Old Testament, God's revealed name is his promise to accompany his people: "I will be with you . . . I will be there for you" (cf. Exodus 3:14). That promise has sounded in every chapter of this book. Thus God always reassures those whom he calls to a particular task when they begin to object that the way is too difficult or that they are not strong enough to endure.

Seven and a half centuries after the Exodus, the same promise came to a defeated, discouraged Israel, weeping "by the waters of Babylon," trying to pick up the pieces of a shattered faith and to cope with a desperate sense of God-forsakenness. The book of Job

is one author's attempt to express this struggle for faith
in the life of an individual. Deutero-Isaiah speaks God's
reassuring word to the disconsolate nation:

> Fear not, for I am with you,
>   be not dismayed, for I am your God;
> I will strengthen you, I will help you,
>   I will uphold you with my
>   victorious right hand.

Isaiah 41:10

> When you pass through the waters
>   I will be with you;
> and through the rivers, they shall
>   not overwhelm you.

Isaiah 43:2

The promise echoes in Paul's speech in Athens: "He is
not far from each one of us, for 'In him we live and move
and have our being' " (Acts 17:27-28). It finds its
fulfillment in the One who is the promise in person:
"Behold, a virgin shall conceive and bear a son, and his
name shall be called Emmanuel (which means, God
with us)" (Matthew 1:23). "Lo, I am with you always, to
the close of the age" (Matthew 28:20).

This is the most startling claim of all regarding God's
providence: that in his unswerving pursuit of his
purposes for humankind, God does not remain aloof.
Because God really is sovereign, he is free to make
himself vulnerable to the worst that evil can do and yet
is able to veto its final triumph. Power that remains
aloof is not as absolute as power that accepts the risks of
involvement with us in order to accompany us into the

deep waters of tragedy and dark valleys of despair and to bring us through them at last.

In the life, death, and resurrection of Jesus Christ, God our keeper faces down the power of evil, sin, and death. In steadfast love God elects to be no more immune than we are from the dangers to love and life which "threaten to undo us"—that is what Emmanuel really means. Notice next time you read them how the Christmas stories emphasize the lowliness of the surroundings (Luke) and the danger to the child (Matthew) as much as the miraculous glory of the event. Notice how over and over again the Gospels show Jesus' confrontation with the powers of destruction and chaos in the form of storms at sea; his confrontation with the power of evil in the temptation stories and the exorcisms; his confrontation with the power of sin in the form of sickness, blindness, and paralysis; and his confrontation with the power of death in the stories of Lazarus and Jairus' daughter. Here is the God who accompanies us to the depths, who, if need be, even descends into hell in order to be God with us. Notice also how the stories of the Passion focus on Jesus' desolation as the end approaches—Gethsemane, the trial, struggling under the weight of the cross, Golgotha. It reaches the depths in the cry of dereliction: "My God, my God, why hast thou forsaken me?" (Matthew 27:46), and ends in a prayer of ultimate confidence: "Father, into thy hands I commit my spirit!" (Luke 23:46).

The God who is our keeper is the God who will not decline the risks of involvement with us here in the heart of darkness, but who accompanies us and gives us the victory "in all these things" (Romans 8:37). God's providence involves not only his eternal preservation of us, but also his presence with us here and now to carry and to save. God keeps us presently, "for *through* him are all things."

IV.

This brings us to the third part of Paul's exclamation: "For . . . *to* him are all things!" This means that God keeps your life surely, not tentatively, not conditionally, not capriciously, but with sure and steadfast affection. The God who preserves and accompanies his creatures and his world cannot and will not be thwarted in his intention to bring all things into conformity to his purposes. Again, the Bible fairly sings of the sovereign rule of God with never any question as to who has the initiative in nature and history or whose hand holds the final power. Come what may, says the Isaiah of the Babylonian exile to his downcast people, God will not lose his grip on you:

> Have you not known? Have you not heard?
> The Lord is the everlasting God,
>   the Creator of the ends of the earth.
> He does not faint or grow weary,
>   his understanding is unsearchable.

Isaiah 40:28

> For the mountains may depart
>   and the hills be removed,

but my steadfast love shall *not*
depart from you.

Having pictured creation as "groaning in travail" as
"God works in all things for good," Paul brings Romans
8 to a stirring crescendo of hope and assurance:

> For I am sure that neither death, nor life, nor angels, nor
> principalities, nor things present, nor things to come, nor
> powers, nor height, nor depth, nor anything else in all
> creation, will be able to separate us from the love of God in
> Christ Jesus our Lord. *(Romans 8:38-39)*

From his Patmos exile, John flings his vision of God's
cosmic victory before the face of a church under
persecution:

> Alleluia: for the Lord God omnipotent reigneth. . . . *(Revelation 19:6 KJV)*

> The kingdom of the world has become the kingdom of our
> Lord and of his Christ, and he shall reign for ever and ever.
> *(Revelation 11:15)*

> King of kings and Lord of lords. *(Revelation 19:16)*

> It is done! I am the Alpha and the Omega, the beginning and
> the end. *(Revelation 21:6)*

Can we still sing with such confidence when there
seems to be so little evidence that God rules the world
with truth and grace? We can, indeed, because we learn
of God's sovereign purpose not from looking first at the
world, but from looking at Jesus Christ. We do not try to

understand God in terms of the world or let the world define God for us. Rather we understand the world in terms of Christ, in whom God presents himself to us and defines his purpose for and among us. Years ago in Robert McAfee Brown's *The Spirit of Protestantism*, I came across an illustrative analogy to which I have returned often in struggling with the difficult question of the rule of grace in the face of the apparent rule of violence and intimidation in the world. J. S. Bach's Passacaglia and Fugue in C Minor consists of a number of variations on a short theme. At first the theme is distinct and clear. As the variations unfold, the music gets more complicated, the theme is increasingly more difficult to distinguish. Soon the music seems to have no direction or purpose whatsoever. However, if you are already acquainted with the theme, you can hear it through all the apparent chaos, holding the music together, giving it direction and force.[3]

The God who preserves and accompanies us, making himself vulnerable even unto death, is also the God who is competent to meet and finally to overcome whatever this world throws at him and at us, by whose side he has graciously chosen to stand. As Albert C. Outler put it in his magnificent Sprunt Lectures on providence, *Who Trusts in God*, the God who is thus sovereign and competent—omnicompetent, if you will—has in love elected to be God with us:

In life's turmoils and drudgery, its vigils and its sunbursts, unraveling and reweaving the strands of our memories and hopes, judging, thwarting, leaving us to suffer for our own misdeeds and those of others and yet never forsaking us even in our sufferings. God-with-us: not to dominate but to bless and yet also to prevent the *final* triumph of our resistance to his righteous rule. God-with-us: endlessly patient, endlessly concerned, endlessly resourceful.[4]

As we extinguish the Advent candles and greet the New Year, we do so in the sure and certain hope that the sovereign God who keeps our life, whose steadfast love endures forever, is present to order and to sustain, to judge and to direct, to forgive and to redeem, concerned above all that our lives come to their intended goals in him. Our keeper is a God who can be worshiped and trusted, who can be questioned and argued with, but who in any case will write the final chapter to the human story and who will provide forever for his children. God keeps you *surely*, "for *to* him are all things."

V.

An old Reformation catechism asks: "What fruit does it yield to know the creation and providence of God?" The answer:

That we should be patient in adversity and thankful in prosperity, and that for the future we should have confidence in our faithful God and Father that no creature will separate us from His love, because all creatures are in His hand, and none can stir or move without His will. (The Heidelberg Catechism, question 28)

The Birth of God

Our congregation has recently discovered a hymn that sets that faith to music. Although a hymn for the New Year, we sing it all year round as a hymn of praise and thanksgiving to God our keeper.

Great God, we sing that mighty hand
By which supported still we stand;
The opening year thy mercy shows,
That mercy crowns it till it close.

With grateful hearts the past we own;
The future, all to us unknown,
We to thy guardian care commit,
And, peaceful, leave before thy feet.

In scenes exalted or depressed,
Thou art our joy, and thou our rest;
Thy goodness all our hopes shall raise,
Adored through all our changing days.

("Great God, We Sing That Mighty Hand")

Seven

Having God on Our Hands

For unto us a child is born, unto us a son is given.

(Isaiah 9:6 KJV)

As Christmas gives way to Epiphany, the strains of a favorite carol linger:

How silently, how silently
The wondrous gift is given!
So God imparts to human hearts
The blessings of his heaven.
No ear may hear his coming,
But in this world of sin,
Where meek souls will receive him, still
The dear Christ enters in.

("O Little Town of Bethlehem")

So, by dark of night, God steals silently down the back way and is born unto us. We take one last, long look at the lovely scene we regularly construct from the birth stories of Luke and Matthew: the holy child in a manger bed, blessed mother Mary, faithful Joseph, the gentle lowly beasts, the humble shepherds, the reverent Magi, the angelic chorus. Usually unpictured, but lurking just ourside, are the dark and hostile forces of "church and state," piety and politics, the "holy" ones and the Herods, the scribes and the Caesars, the priests and the Pilates, all "vexed to nightmare by a rocking cradle" (Yeats). The words come back to us:

And the word became flesh. *(I John 1:14)*

To you is born a Savior. *(Luke 2:11)*

And his name shall be Emmanuel—God with us. *(Matthew 1:23)*

This is my beloved Son. *(Matthew 3:17; cf. Mark 1:11)*

So what now? What will you do with him? Those are the questions Epiphany poses.

We should have known—we have known all along, have we not?—that the event we have anticipated, prepared for, and celebrated was going to involve us in a rather significant way. The note sounded early on in Isaiah's advent prophecy:

For to us a child is born,
    to us a son is given;
and the government will be upon
        his shoulder,
    and his name will be called
"Wonderful Counselor, Mighty God,
    Everlasting Father, Prince of Peace."

Of the increase of his government
    and of peace
   there will be no end,
upon the throne of David, and over
    his kingdom,
   to establish it, and to uphold it
with justice and with righteousness
   from this time forth and for evermore.
The zeal of the Lord of hosts will do this.

                        Isaiah 9:6-7

Unto us. Does Christmas mean not only that God has taken our lives into his hands, but also that we now have God on our hands? Has God actually linked his cause and his kingdom to us? What if it is *unto us* that a child is born and a son is given? What might it mean, individually and in our life together, to be responsible and to be held responsible for this One born "unto us"?

I.

First of all, having God on our hands means that we have a responsibility to receive God with worship and reverence. At its deepest level, it is the responsibility to proclaim and to demonstrate a God-consciousness within human life, a Christ-perspective upon human affairs, a faith dimension to human existence.

A central theme of biblical faith is the conviction that, as Hebrews 4:13 expresses it, every human being has to do with the living God. You and I are created for God. Belonging to God is not merely an option we may or may not exercise; it is the first and final fact of human life—a fact which we may deny, as many people do, but one that we cannot change. When Augustine prayed, "Thou hast made us for Thyself, and our hearts are restless till they rest in Thee," he expressed the biblical insight that to be human is to be a man or a woman responsible before God, by whose intention and in whose image we are made.

To be responsible to God, in whose providence and grace there is born "unto us" a child, a son, a Savior, means, therefore, to live in an attitude of reverence. It means to live, not self-consciously or self-righteously, but quietly confident of the presence and providence of God in and over all of life. Commenting on the religious and moral climate of our time, James Gustafson wrote:

> What is deficient in the pieties and moral disciplines of contemporary church life is what Calvin and the Reformed Tradition have accented with particular strength, namely a theocentric focus for all of life: that vital sense of dependence upon the sustaining power and mercy of God; that vital sense of human limits and realism about human corruption (including and especially our own) in the face of the holiness of God; that vital sense of the *telos*, the end, to which all life is lived and ordered—the grateful celebration and glorification of the majestic power that creates, sustains, limits, and creates possibilities for all of life in the creation.[1]

Of course, there are those who do not agree that life is God-centered or that human beings belong to and are responsible to God. It is entirely possible to disdain the consciousness of God in one's life. It is easy enough to live, practically and politically, as if there were no God who sees and cares how we treat people, what our concerns really are, and what we give ourselves to. Perhaps the smartest thing to do after all is just to follow our ambition to its conclusion. Or is that smart after all?

In Luke's Gospel, when Mary is told that she will bear a son who will be the Savior, she sings: "[God] has put down the mighty from their thrones, and exalted those of low degree" (Luke 1:52). How does God do that? How does this "putting down" happen in history, in the life of the individual, and in the life of a nation? Perhaps God puts down the mighty simply by turning away from them. Is that not the most terrible thing God can do to us, to let us do what we want to do? What would be worse than to arrive at our personal goals—to enjoy at last social standing, to exercise political influence, to attain professional, vocational, academic, and religious summits we have spent ourselves and even sacrificed to reach—and find that God has not been a part of it? Could that be the meaning of damnation, of hell, when our goals are reached, when we "make it" without God?[2] In his poem "Well?" G. A. Studdert-Kennedy tells of a young cockney lad who, having lived for self into early adulthood, looks back in a dream over his empty, wasted life. In agony of soul, the young man notices a figure standing beside him, in whose eyes are God's own pain and heartache. For a long time the figure stares at him silently and then says just one word: "Well?" After he awakens, the young man tells his friends of his encounter with judgment.

The Birth of God

For I daren't face in the land o' grace
The sorrow o' those eyes . . .
And, boys, I'd sooner frizzle up,
I' the flames of a burnin' 'Ell,
Than stand and look into 'Is face,
And 'ear 'Is voice say—"Well?"[3]

from *The Unutterable Beauty*, Harper & Brothers, 1936.

II.

Second, having God on our hands means that we
have a responsibility to and for one another.

In his Christmas oratorio, "For the Time Being," W.
H. Auden speaks of "the stable where for once in our
lives/Everything became a You and nothing was an It."[4]
The birth of this child "unto us" gives us unto one
another in a communion that he will henceforth
mediate and to which his own spirit of love and
compassion, justice and generosity, grace and goodwill
is the clue and the key.

What this call to compassion and goodwill means for
you and me personally is for each of us individually and
in our life together to "work out . . . with fear and
trembling" (cf. Philippians 2:12). This much, however,
is certain: In times of growing insecurity, when money
gets tighter and we begin to fret and when fear is on the
increase, with neighborhood burglaries almost a daily
occurrence and when national security is shakier than it
has been in a long time—in times such as these,
compassion, goodwill, and generosity are in increasingly short supply. The willingness to bear one

another's burdens is often replaced by a frantic pursuit of personal security and a corresponding hardness of will and coldness of heart toward the poor, the ignorant, and the downtrodden.

We in the Christian community might ask ourselves: To what persons, to what institutions, to what communities will our society and our world in the years ahead be able to look for compassion and comfort, justice and love? From what institutions will such light shine into the darkness of a world that has other fish to fry just now? Might that just be the responsibility and opportunity of the church of Jesus Christ?

Even dedicated Christian leaders have been discouraged from such hope. The late Dean William R. Inge is reported to have said that institutional religion does not represent the gospel of Christ but the opinions of a mass of nominal Christians, and cannot be expected to do more than to look after its own interests and reflect the ideas of its supporters. As pastors and congregations, we need to hear that indictment. We need to be warned that churches that always seek their own good usually end up with more respectability and less righteousness, more property and less passion, more numbers and fewer disciples, more money and less faith, more success and less sanctity, more security and less courage. And down the road they find themselves asking: "Lord, when did we see thee hungry or thirsty or a stranger or naked or sick or in prison, and did not minister to thee?" Each year. at budget time, church officers struggle with the issue of expenses and benevolences. One elder, himself a very generous man, has a way of reminding us of God's call to an outreach of compassion and generosity. "Now remember," he says, "we want to be a giving church, not just a spending church."

The commitment to compassion and justice does not call for a new kind of "double predestination" in which, by the definition of current ideology, God is always for the poor and weak and always against the wealthy and strong. It is simply not true that the only faithful way to read the Bible is through the eyes of the poor (not even "liberation theology" can be allowed to take the Bible captive). The gospel as the power of God for salvation reaches to depths of human existence and circumstance far beyond those described in physical or economic terms. But we, whose responsibility it is to preach the word of God and to interpret the faith of the church, must not ignore the fact that the law, the prophets, the Gospels, and the Epistles call attention in a special way to the poor and their needs. The cry for compassion and mercy on the part of those on whom life presses down is the first word that covenanted and redeemed people must hear as a test of their worship and as an expression of their faith in him who is born unto us as Lord and Savior, and upon whose shoulders is a government established and upheld with justice and righteousness and peace.

III.

Finally, to have God on our hands means that we have a moral responsibility to and for our world, that it may increasingly become and continue as a place safe and fit for future generations. Given the shape of our world today, no issues are more immediately in need of the attention of the people of God and the perspective of Christian faith and values than those of world hunger and peace.

No doubt we have often heard it said: "But those are political matters on which we could never all agree. We just have to leave all that to the politicians and generals." However, if it is true that "The earth is the Lord's and the fulness thereof, the world and those who dwell therein" (Psalm 24:1), then the world does not belong to governments or armies, but to One who made it and who made us to live in it, and who, to the best of our knowledge, does not want his children to starve or his world destroyed.

Christian citizens differ over the causes and cures of hunger and over the preferred stockpile of weapons and the size of national defense budgets (or over having weapons and defense budgets at all, as in the case of pacifists). With a nuclear holocaust and nuclear winter only minutes away from a pushed button or a malfunctioning computer, we can hardly afford the luxury of impugning one another's motives in our various proposals for lasting peace and effective security.

Consider, however, that the United Nations reports that its 3.2 billion dollar total budget for humanitarian programs, such as UNICEF, UNESCO and others, is dwarfed by the almost 900 billion dollars its member nations spend on arms! Surely the one born unto us as

Prince of peace sits in judgment of such cynical priorities! Surely Christian values and biblical faith urge us toward, and not away from, attitudes and actions that put a priority on the reduction of arms expenditures, the defusing of nuclear weapons, and the curbing of violence within and among nations.

Twenty-five years ago it was determined that if America had 200 to 400 warheads that would be enough to kill one-third of the Russian people. Surely the Soviet Union also knew what it would take to kill one-third of the American people. Twenty-five years later we can be even more "effective" against one another. But such talk is immoral, obscene! If anybody had talked of killing one-third of the population of any country at the beginning of this century, that person would have been put in a mental institution. Today in the Soviety Union, anyone who protests *against* such obscenity is put in an institution. Anyone doing so in America is frequently put down as naïve at best and unpatriotic at worst. Yet a handful of people have brought our world to this point.

The psalmist wrote: "The heavens are the Lord's heavens, but the earth he has given to the sons of men" (Psalm 115:16). My God, what if he has? What in God's name is our responsibility to God's human and cosmic creation? As I think about the hopes and commitments within my own congregation and my own family, it strikes me that it really does not matter very much that we learn to produce more food and end famine if nuclear war is going to turn the sun from a source of life into an instrument of death. It matters little that we get an education and find a good job and make money and work for better schools and wipe out slums and clean up the environment and make our cities more humane. It matters little that we do research, cure cancer, preach sermons, send out missionaries, grow in faith, minister to the community, have children, or play Mozart if it all is going to end with a bang *and* a whimper. However variously situated committed Christian people are along the ideological spectrum, surely our prior commitment is to put our faith and values into practice by trying to translate them into attitudes and policies of justice and peace. However vigorously engaged we are in the pursuit of a preferred political and economic vision, surely our prior engagement is toward a world in which, according to another of Isaiah's advent visions, "They shall not hurt or destroy in all [God's] holy mountain" (Isaiah 11:9*a*). That is to say, world hunger and peace are theological issues long before, and long after, they are political, military, economic, or ideological issues.

In any case, that this child is born unto us means that God has played his hand and has called our hand in this matter of involvement with and responsibility to the world. As William Temple reminded us:

> It was into the real world that Christ came, into the city where there was no room for Him, and into a country where Herod, the murderer of innocents, was king. He comes to us, not to shield us from the harshness of the world, but to give us the courage and strength to bear it; not to snatch us away by some miracle from the conflict of life, but to give us peace . . . His peace . . . in our hearts, by which we may be calmly steadfast while the conflict rages, and be able to bring to the torn world the healing that is peace.

IV.

So by dark of night, God steals silently down the back way and is born unto us. What might it mean for the undoing and redoing of our lives, our nation's life, and our world view that we are responsible for this One born unto us, that we shall be held responsible for his cause in the earth? We like the part about Christmas' meaning that we are in God's hands. But the part about having God on our hands is not so easy to deal with or to live with.

What would be more difficult, however, would be to have God off our hands, to be left to live, love, work, struggle, rejoice, weep, hope, and die without God. It helps to hold faith and life together to remember that part of this coming "unto us" of a Savior was the flight of the holy family into Egypt in the face of Herod's rage. The French artist Luc Olivier Merson captured the scene in a painting, "Repose in Egypt," which shows Mary and the child asleep in the hollow between the body and the right paw of the Sphinx. The painting reminds us that the enigma of life remains; it is well typified by the Sphinx and by the cruelty of Herod. We live our lives under a vast question mark, what Wordsworth called, "the burthen of the Mystery . . . of all the unintelligible world" ("Lines Composed a Few Miles Above Tintern Abbey"). The Sphinx symbolizes that question mark. It symbolizes also the contradictions in human beings, who sometimes seem a mixture of serpent, winged beast, lion, and man. But if the Sphinx remains, it is also our faith that the Christ child is born and sleeps peacefully between the lion's paws![5]

As for our making any difference as Christian people in a world so much more committed to violence than to compassion, here is something to consider: When we were children, we heard stories of the prehistoric monsters that once roamed the earth, and we wondered how mere human beings could ever have disposed of them. When we grew older we discovered the answer: the climate changed, and the monsters died. Who knows what might happen to a world in the grip of violence and fear if the church really set about to change the climate?

Perhaps the final verse of that favorite, lingering carol is an appropriate Epiphany prayer of invocation and welcome to the One born "unto us":

O holy Child of Bethlehem,
Descend to us, we pray;
Cast out our sin, and enter in,
Be born in us today.
We hear the Christmas angels
The great glad tidings tell;
O come to us, abide with us,
Our Lord Emmanuel.

("O Little Town of Bethlehem")

Notes

Preface

1. Donald G. Miller, former president of Pittsburg Theological Seminary where Markus Barth had been a member of the faculty, told of this letter in an address to the Candidates Committee of Mecklenburg Presbytery, Charlotte, N.C., December 30, 1975.

2. For two different overtures to such a project in biblical theology, see Claus Westermann, *What Does the Old Testament Say About God?* (Atlanta: John Knox Press, 1979) and Samuel Terrien, *The Elusive Presence; Toward a New Biblical Theology* (San Francisco: Harper & Row, 1978).

3. John H. Leith, ed., *Creeds of the Churches*, rev. ed. (Atlanta: John Knox Press, 1982), p. 1.

4. In addition to Barth's *Church Dogmatics*, his well-known *The Humanity of God*, *The Great Promise* (an exposition of Luke 1), and a collection of Christmas meditations written for German daily newspapers, entitled simply *Christmas*, I would call particular attention to his earlier essays collected in the volume

The Word of God and the Word of Man, which have an uncanny contemporaneity for the theological situation in the United States more than half a century after their publication in Europe.

5. For a useful and much wider discussion of hymnody, poetry, and preaching, see Elizabeth Achtemeier's "The Use of Hymnic Elements in Preaching," *Interpretation* (January 1985), p. 46.

1. The Encompassing Mystery

1. John Baillie, *The Idea of Revelation in Recent Thought* (New York: Columbia University Press, 1956), p. 27.

2. John S. Whale, *Christian Doctrine* (London: Cambridge University Press, 1941), p. 32.

3. Paul Scherer, *Event in Eternity* (New York: Harper and Bros., 1945), p. 36.

4. Ibid., p. 67.

5. H. Richard Niebuhr, *The Meaning of Revelation* (New York: Macmillan, 1960), p. 36.

6. See Karl Barth, *Church Dogmatics* vol. III, part 1 (Edinburgh: T. & T. Clark, 1958), p. 67.

7. See Scherer, *Event*, p. 103.

2. The Mystery Set Forth in Christ

1. T. S. Eliot, *The Complete Poems and Plays* (New York: Harcourt, Brace and World, 1952), p. 107.

2. Niebuhr, *The Meaing of Revelation*, p. 93.
3. Bertrand Russell, *Why I Am Not a Christian* (New York: Simon & Schuster, 1957), p. 113.
4. Scherer, *Event*, p. 40.

3. The Birth of God

1. Karl Barth, *Fragments Grave and Gay* (London: Collins, 1971), p. 17.

4. The Beyond in the Midst of Life (God with Us)

1. William Temple, *The Preacher's Theme Today* (London: S.P.C.K., 1936), pp. 31-32.

5. Be Not Afraid

1. W. H. Auden, "For the Time Being: A Christmas Oratorio" in *Religious Drama*, vol. 1, ed. Marvin Halverson (Cleveland: The World Publishing Company, 1957), p. 66.

6. The Keeper of Your Life

1. Marc Connelly, *The Green Pastures* (New York: Reinhart & Co., 1929), pp. 28 ff.
2. Barth, *Church Dogmatics*, vol. III, part 3, p. 90.

3. Robert M. Brown, *The Spirit of Protestantism* (New York: Oxford University Press, 1961), p. 82.

4. Albert C. Outler, *Who Trusts in God* (New York: Oxford University Press, 1968), pp. 105-6.

7. Having God on Our Hands

1. James Gustafson, "The Nature of the Ministry from a Reformed Perspective," a paper delivered October 18, 1979, at McCormick Theological Seminary in Chicago (cited by Browne Barr in *The Christian Century* [November 26, 1980], p. 1160).

2. See Barth, *The Great Promise* (New York: The Philosophical Library, 1963), p. 53.

3. G. A. Studdert-Kennedy, *The Best of G. A. Studdert-Kennedy, Selected from His Writings by a Friend* (New York: Harper and Bros., 1924), p. 164.

4. Auden, "For the Time Being," *Religious Drama*, p. 67.

5. See George A. Buttrick, *The Interpreter's Bible*, vol. 7, G. A. Buttrick, ed. (Nashville: Abingdon-Cokesbury Press, 1951), p. 260.

Bibliography

Alston, Wallace M., Jr. *The Church*. Atlanta: John Knox Press, 1984.

Auden, W. H. "For the Time Being: A Christmas Oratorio" in *Religious Drama*, vol. I, ed. Marvin Halverson. Cleveland: The World Publishing Company, 1957.

Baillie, D. M. *God Was in Christ*. New York: Faber & Faber, 1977.

Baillie, John. *The Idea of Revelation in Recent Thought*. New York: Columbia University Press, 1956.

Barth, Karl. *Christmas*. London: Oliver and Boyd, 1959.

———. *Church Dogmatics*, vol. I, parts 1 and 2; vol. II, part 2; vol. III, parts 1 and 3; vol. IV, parts 1 and 2. Edinburgh: T. & T. Clark, 1958.

———. *Credo*. New York: Charles Scribner's Sons, 1962.

———. *Fragments Grave and Gay*. London: Collins Pubs., 1976.

———. *The Great Promise*. New York: The Philosophical Library, 1963.

————. *The Humanity of God*. Atlanta: John Knox Press, 1960.

————. *The Word of God and the Word of Man*. New York: Harper, 1928.

Bonhoeffer, Dietrich. *Christ the Center*. New York: Harper & Row, 1978.

————. *Letters and Papers from Prison*. New York: Macmillan, 1972.

The Book of Confessions. New York: The Office of the General Assembly of The Presbyterian Church (U.S.A.), 1983.

Brown, Raymond E. *The Birth of the Messiah*. Garden City, N.Y.: Doubleday, 1977.

Brown, Robert McAfee. *The Spirit of Protestantism*. New York: Oxford University Press, 1965.

Buttrick, George A., ed. *The Interpreter's Bible*, vol. 7. Nashville: Abingdon Press, 1951.

Connelly, Marc. *The Green Pastures*. New York: Reinhart & Co., 1929.

Eliot, T. S. *The Complete Poems and Plays, 1909-1950*. New York: Harcourt, Brace and World, 1952.

Forsyth, Peter T. *The Person and Place of Jesus Christ*. Grand Rapids, Mich.: Wm. B. Eerdmans Publishing Company. (The American edition is reprinted from the Third Edition published by Congregational Union of England and Wales and Hodder & Stoughton, London.)

————. *Positive Preaching and the Modern Mind*. New York: Baker Books, 1980.

Leith, John H. *An Introduction to the Reformed Tradition*. Atlanta: John Knox Press, 1981.

————, ed. *Creeds of the Churches*, rev. ed. Atlanta: John Knox Press, 1982.

McCabe, Joseph E. *Handel's Messiah: A Devotional Commentary*. Philadelphia: The Westminster Press, 1978.

Niebuhr, H. Richard. *The Meaning of Revelation*. New York: Macmillan, 1960.

Niebuhr, Reinhold, *The Nature and Destiny of Man*, two volumes. New York: Charles Scribner's Sons, 1964.

Outler, Albert C. *Who Trusts in God*. New York: Oxford University Press, 1968.

Russell, Bertrand. *Why I Am Not a Christian*. New York: Simon & Schuster, 1967.

Scherer, Paul. *Event in Eternity*. New York: Harper and Bros., 1945.

Studdert-Kennedy, G. A. *The Best of G. A. Studdert-Kennedy*, New York: Harper and Bros., 1924.

Temple, William. *Christus Veritas*. London: Macmillan, 1930.

————. *Mens Creatrix*. London: Macmillan, 1949.

————. *Nature, Man, and God*. New York: AMS Press, 1979.

————. *The Preacher's Theme Today*. London: S.P.C.K., 1936.

Terrien, Samuel. *The Elusive Presence: Toward a New Biblical Theology*. San Francisco: Harper & Row, 1978.

Von Rad, Gerhard. *Genesis: A Commentary*. Philadelphia: The Westminster Press, 1973.

Westermann, Claus. *What Does The Old Testament Say about God?* Atlanta: John Knox Press, 1979.

Whale, John S. *Christian Doctrine*. London: Cambridge University Press, 1941.